To: Gabriel &
From: Martha & Hank

Bruce E. Gwodoer 2/10/2019

Library of Congress
ISSN 2169-8139

My Wild Animal Friends ™ A-Z

by Bruce E. Meadows

First Edition
Copyright@2013 by Meadows Photography - Publisher
Cincinnati, Ohio

email: mywildanimalfriends@fuse.net
Gallery: www.wildaboutphotos.smugmug.com
website: mywildanimalfriends.com

Damara Dik-Dik

Dedicated to my beloved spouse,

Joan, who has been my partner,

best friend, confidant for over 44 years.

Without her traveling with me through

this journey of life this book would not exist.

Master of Art in Art Education - University of Cincinnati
Bachelor of Fine Art in Photography - Miami University

Bruce E. Meadows
Photographer, Teacher, Artist, Author, Illustrator

" As a teacher and naturalist I have a deep passion to help students understand the world around them. Animals like people have personalities, my book was designed with this thought in mind. I hope you will walk away enlightened and enriched."

The majority of the photographs in this book were taken by the author, using a: Nikon D2Xs and a Nikon 80-400VR lens.

Robert Russell, PhD "He is compassionate and patient with his students, a passionate advocate for them, and committed to excellence in teaching. Bruce combined both caring and commitment to foster learning and a positive rapport with his students."

Flavia Bastos, PhD "He strives to deliver his best academic performance in all situations. His back-ground also enriches his teaching persona, creating an aura of knowledge and respect that draws students' attention. He has leavened his coursework with his rich personal experiences, and many times served as a role model for the less experienced students in our program."

Table of Contents

I am an **Ape**, not a monkey because I have NO tail and can stand upright!

My name: **Western Silverback Gorilla** (scientific name: *Gorilla gorilla.*) I am the dominant male of my troop.

- As a species we are the largest primates in the world. Although I look fierce, I am shy and peaceful except when protecting my family from a rival male or humans. When this happens I beat my chest, act wildly and make terrifying hoots ending in a loud roar which will make the hair stand up on the back of your neck.

I am a Female Gorilla
Hooray for woman power!

- We like to take a siesta in the late afternoon in a nest of branches and leaves.
- We are great climbers, and use our hands and feet to climb and swing though the trees. We are among the most intelligent of all animals and eat plants, stems, leaves, and berries. We are categorized into two groups:
  1. Lesser Apes (gibbons)
  2. Great Apes (orangutans, gorillas, and chimpanzees)

All gorillas are on the endangered species list because our forest homes are being cut down (called deforestation).

Western Lowland Silverback Gorilla

Here are some interesting facts about my species:

- We have very long arms, stretching from 7.5 to 8.5 ft. (2.3 to 2.6 m.)

- When we walk, our body weight is pressed down on the ground through our knuckles. This is called **Knuckle-walking**.

- Our natural habitat covers tropical or subtropical forests in Africa and a wide range of elevations ranging in altitude from 7,200-14,100 ft. (2,200-4,300 m.) My lowland gorilla friends live in dense forests and lowland swamps and marshes as low as sea level.

- We live in groups called **troops**, and as the dominant male I am its leader. As the center of the troop's attention, I am responsible for making all decisions, mediating conflicts, determining the movements of the group, leading the troop to feeding sites, and the safety and well-being of the troop.

I am very intelligent! Who am I?

I am an Ape too!
My name: Sumatran Orangutan

- Like all apes I have no tail.

- As you can see, I am very hairy.

- I am considered one of the most intelligent animals on earth and use tools to make my life easier.

- **To keep cool I shade my head from the sun with this piece of cardboard.**

- I can break off a tree branch snap off the twigs and fray one end, then use it to stick in tree holes so that termites will come out for me to eat. This method also works in bee hives as I search for the bee's sweet honey!

- My habitat is being destroyed by deforestation, and we are critically endangered, with less than 7,000 left in the wild.

- Male Orangutans grow to about 4.6 ft. tall (1.4 m) and 200 lbs. (90 kg.) Females are smaller.

- I prefer eating fruits like figs and jackfruits, but sometimes eat bird eggs and small vertebrates.

- I am indigenous to the island of Sumatra, and named after this island. Masses of us gather on the northern part of the island to feed on the fruiting fig trees.

I am a Bat (Scientific name: *Chiroptera*) from the Greek word *cheir*, "hand" and *pteron*, "wing".

My forelimbs form webbed wings, making me the only mammal naturally capable of true and sustained flight.

- There are about 1,240 bat species in the world, making us about 20% of all classified mammal species worldwide.

- I sleep upside down, and live mostly in tropical forests and caves.

- I am good for the environment as I help pollinate flowers, trees, cacti, avocados, bananas, breadfruit, dates, figs, mangoes, peaches. and disperse fruit seeds.

- Some of us prefer to eat fruit, nectar or pollen while others prefer insects and other pests. I can eat half my weight in insects each night. About 70% of us are insectivores, most of the rest are frugivores or fruit eaters.

- When I fly, I make a high-pitch sound which bounces off objects and returns to me as echoes. I can distinguish the difference in sound between a tree, your head, or a tasty grasshopper.

- I have great night vision but am color blind and only see in black, white, and shades of gray.

- The largest of our species is the flying fox *Pteropus*, with a wingspan of up to 6 feet (1.8 m.)

- Over 60 of our species are listed as endangered.

I am the **Polar Bear**, King of the Artic (scientific name: *Ursus maritimus* Latin for maritime bear since I spend many months of the year at sea.)

- I am the largest land carnivore in the world, I can grow to a weight of more than 1,400 pounds (females are much lighter with an average girl weighing around 400 lbs.)

- I have transparent fur over my black skin which absorbs heat. Reflection of the sunlight from the densely packed transparent hairs makes me appear to be white. My fur is made up of hollow hairs called guard hairs. These air-filled guard hairs help transmit heat from the sunlight and my black skin acts as a solar heat collector. In turn, the reflection stops the heat being lost from my skin.

- Under my skin is almost 4 inches of blubber (fat) which insulates me from sub-zero temperatures.

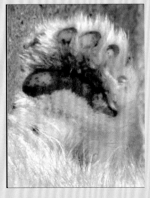

- I have 42 teeth which are needed for my carnivorous diet of seals and salmon. I sometimes eat berries and rodents during the summer and have been known to snack on walruses, whales, seabirds, and even caribou.

- I am a very strong swimmer, and use my large webbed front paws to paddle. My fur is waterproof which helps keep me warm in the cold Artic water.

- My closest relative is the **Kodiak brown bear** or the **Alaskan grizzly bear**.

I am a Bactrian Camel

(scientific name: *Camelus bactrianus*)

Did you know camels (also called Camelids) have either one or two humps? I am sometimes confused with the Arabian camel who has one hump, I have two.

- I live an average of 40 to 50 years. Fully grown I can stand 7 feet 1 inch (1.85 m) tall at the top of my hump and weigh up to 1,500 pounds (690 kg). As a sprint runner, I can reach speeds to 40 mph (65 km/h). *Camelids* have a funny rocking walk, moving both left legs together, then the right legs together which is known as "pacing".

- I can drink up to 40 gallons (150 liters) of water, but do not store water in my hump(s) as humans commonly believe. Humps are reservoirs of fatty tissue that when metabolized provide a source of energy yielding more than one gallon of water for each gallon of fat. I can survive without water for up to two months.

- Scientists believe that our ancestors migrated from North America to Asia across the Bering Strait (temporary land bridge) 60 million years ago. We are primarily domesticated animals which have been reintroduced into the wild.

- My bushy eyebrows and two rows of long eyelashes protect my eyes from the hot desert sun. My large, tough lips enable me to pick at dry, thorny desert vegetation, and my huge thick footpads help me navigate the rough rocky terrain and shifting desert sands.

I am a **Cheetah** (scientific name: *Acinonyx jubatus*) I am the fastest living land animal on the planet! In the wild I can run 65 mph (104 km/h.) A Cheetah from the Cincinnati Zoo set a world best time: 100 meters in 5.7 seconds *(see Appendix on pg. 54).*

- My semi-retractable claws with pads disallow gripping, I do not climb upright trees well, but to eat I will take my meal into the tree branches to keep other scavengers away.

- When I run, my large nostrils allow for increased oxygen intake, and my enlarged heart and lungs work together to circulate oxygen efficiently to help me run at blazing speeds.

I make a wide variety of noises called vocalizations, as listed below:

- **Chirping**: When a cheetah attempts to find another, or a mother tries to locate her cubs, it uses a high-pitched barking called chirping. The chirps made by a cheetah cub sound more like a bird chirping, and so are termed chirping, too.

- **Churring** or **stuttering**: This vocalization is emitted by a cheetah during social meetings. A churr can be seen as a social invitation to other cheetahs, an expression of interest, uncertainty, or appeasement or during meetings with the opposite sex (although each sex churrs for different reasons).

- **Growling**: This vocalization is often accompanied by hissing and spitting and is exhibited by the cheetah during annoyance, or when faced with danger.

- **Yowling**: This is an escalated version of growling, usually displayed when danger worsens.

- **Agonistic vocalizations**: a combination of growls, moans, hisses and the "trademark" cheetah spit, which is most often accompanied by a forceful "paw hit" on the ground.

- **Purring**: This is made when the cheetah is content, usually during pleasant social meetings (mostly between cubs and their mothers).
  (SOURCE: Wikipedia)

I am an Australian Dingo

(scientific name: *Canis lupus dingo.*)

I am a free roaming wild dog unique to the continent of Australia, mainly found in the outback.

- Our natural habitat can range from deserts, to grasslands and on the verge of forests. We can not live too far away from water and normally settle our homes in dens, deserted rabbit holes, and hollow logs.

- Our average weight is 29 to 44 pounds (13 to 20 kg); however, there are a few records of weights up to 60 to 77 pounds (27 to 35 kg.)

- We tend to howl and whimper, and bark less than domestic dogs. Our howling, which includes moans, bark-howl, and snuffs, have at least 10 variations of howling which varies depending on the time of day and the season. Our vocalizations are influenced by breeding, migration, lactation, social stability, and behavior. Our howling is more frequent when we are short of food. We enjoy howling as a group .

- Aside from vocal communication, we communicate like the domestic dog, by **scent-marking** specific objects. We also **scent-rub**. Have you ever seen a dog roll on its neck, shoulders, or back on something that is usually associated with food or the scent markings of other dogs or animals? We do that too!

- Like many wild animals, in order to survive we are hunters. When hunting larger prey we form a group hunt. Such group formations are unnecessary when hunting rabbits or other small prey.

- We are generally highly social animals and form stable packs with clearly defined territories, which only rarely overlap with the territories of neighboring packs.

Yes, I'm a **Donkey**, but my wild animal name is **African Wild Ass**
(scientific name: *Equus africanus*)

As a species we are herbivores and spend our time grazing on grasses, but we also eat scrub, bark, and tough desert plants. Our ancestor is believed to be the domestic donkey.

- We live in the deserts and other arid areas of the Horn of Africa, Eritrea, Ethiopia and Somalia.

- We are well suited to life in a desert or semi-desert environment as we have tough digestive systems, which can break down desert vegetation and extract moisture from food efficiently. We can go without water for a fairly long time. Our large ears give us an excellent sense of hearing and help in keeping us cool.

We are the Elephants (scientific species name: *Elephantidae*)

- We are the largest living land animals on Earth today. How large can we get?

- The largest male African Elephant weighs as much as this HIMARS vehicle which weighs 24,000lb. (10,900 kg.) The elephant is often taller than the HIMARS, 13 ft.

- We talk to one another by making loud rumbling and growling noises with our stomachs that other elephants can hear.

- Our brains are the largest of all land animals.

- We can remember how to find food and watering holes that are great distances away.

- If an old watering hole appears dry, we have learned how to dig a well *(National Geographic Kids March 2009.)*

- At birth, I weigh about 230 pounds (105 kg) and stand about 3 feet tall.

- I typically live for 50 to 70 years, but have been known to live as long as 82 years.

- I have a big appetite and eat all types of vegetation, from grass and fruit to leaves and bark, about 220 to 440 pounds (100 to 200 kg) each day. I poop about 200 lbs. of manure.

- As a full grown healthy adult I have no natural predators, with one exception: MAN. I am poached for my valuable tusks which are traded illegally to make all kinds of ornaments and medicines.

- My ears (shaped like the country of Africa) act like air conditioners. As I flap my wet ears on a hot day, the blood flowing through the many blood vessels is cooled. This in turn cools my large body.

- **How smart am I?** Smart enough to pick up a tree branch with my trunk to shoo away flies and pesky insects.

Just having a little fun with my friends!

I am another kind of elephant, an **Elephant Seal** (scientific name: *Mirounga*), also called a Sea Elephant. The largest sea mammal that comes ashore to breed.

- We are at home on the coasts of Mexico and southern California,

- We are divided into two species: Northern elephant seals can be found in California and Baja California and Southern elephant seals living in sub-Antarctic and Antarctic waters. Although it is brutally cold we are shielded from the extremely cold water by our blubber. We thrive in the artic water because it is rich in fish, squid, and other marine foods love to eat.

- Southern elephants are the largest of all seals. Males can be over 20 feet long (6 m) and weigh up to 8,800 pounds (4,000 kg.) These massive pinnipeds are not called elephant seals because of their size. They get their name from their trunk-like inflatable snouts.

- Females have an eleven month pregnancy and give birth in late winter to a single pup which is nursed for approximately one month. While suckling their young, females do not eat; both mother and child live off the energy stored in ample reserves of her blubber.

- As a male I have a huge *proboscis* (nose.) It is filled with cavities designed to reabsorb moisture from my breath. This is important during the mating season because we do not leave the beach to feed and need to conserve our body moisture though our noses as we have no other source of water.

- My roar can be heard from several miles away.

We are **Flamingos** (scientific name: ***Phoenicopterus*** from Greek word φοινικόπτερος means "purple wing")

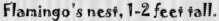
Flamingo's nest, 1-2 feet tall.

- We get our beautiful orange/pink color from the Carotenoids in crustaceans we eat, which may be blue or green, but after being digested become orange/pink and are deposited in our growing feathers. We are the only birds that filter our food by pumping water through slits in our beaks and tongue.

- We come in four flamingo species in the Americas and two in the *Old World*. (The *Old World* comprises Africa, Asia, and Europe, the *New World* refers to the Western Hemisphere, primarily North and South America.)

- We are very social birds and live in colonies that can number in the thousands.

- We often stand on one leg, the other tucked beneath our body. The picture on the top left shows us standing both ways.

- As you can see by the above picture we build our nest on a mudflat high enough to keep the water and predators away. We viciously defend our nesting sites and young.

- When chicks are born, both Mom and Dad share in feeding milk to the young (for most of the animal kingdom it is Mom's job.) Our milk also contains red and white blood cells.

- Ancient Egyptians considered Flamingos to be the living representation of the god Ra.

- As one of the oldest species of birds our fossil remains date back 30 to 50 million years.

- *I am the elusive* **Red Fox** (scientific name: ***Vulpes vulpes***) Our species is the largest and most widespread fox.

- I can be found in the Northern Hemisphere from the Arctic Circle to North Africa, Central America and Asia. Forty five sub-species have been recognized.

- I primarily feed on small rodents, sometimes target game birds, reptiles, invertebrates and young ungulates (small mammals like rabbits), and on occasion eat fruits and vegetables.

- My tail is unusual because it is longer than half my body length.

- Fox fur ranges in color, and may be white, gray, silver, platinum, amber, red, blackish-brown, and samson (black.)

- Our dens are underground, and we can have up to 12 cubs in a litter. Both parents help look after the cubs.

We are **Gibbons** (scientific family name: *Hylobatidae*), as members of the Ape family we have no tail!

- We are the animals people think of as primates swinging gracefully through the rain forest, We rarely descend to the ground.

- We are Omnivores, from the Latin words: omni, meaning "all, everything"; vorare, "to devour".) We eat both plants and animal material as our primary food sources.

- We are the fastest and most agile of all tree-dwelling, non-flying mammals.

- We swing from branch to branch for distances of up to 50 ft. (15 m), at speeds as high as 35 mph (56 km/h.)

- Unlike other apes, we display pair-bonding (only one male to one female.)

- Our fur coloration varies from dark to light brown shades, and anywhere between black and white.

- All but one of our 15 species is listed as critically endangered.

I am a white cheeked "Crested"

Gibbon (scientific name: *Nomascus leucogenys*)

- Both males and females have unusually long arms, even for gibbons, with the arms being 1.2 to 1.4 times longer than our legs.

- I am generally sociable, living in groups of up to six individuals. Individual groups do not travel far.

- The Northern White Cheeked Gibbon is black with white.

I am a Sumali Giraffe or Reticulated Giraffe (scientific name: *Giraffa camelopardalis reticulate*)

- I am the most common Giraffe, with polygonal liver-colored spots which cover my body and legs. There are nine subspecies of Giraffes.

- The Nigerian Giraffe and the Rothschild Giraffe usually have no spots below the knee cap, and the Rothschild Giraffe is the only species born with five horns, most Giraffes have only two. The Thornicroft Giraffe have numerous pale yellowish/red star shaped spots.

- I am the tallest terrestrial (land) animal in the world.

- What is my six foot neck good for? I can easily snatch a snack high up in the trees where other animals can't reach.

- My long legs allow me to run as fast as 35 mph (56 km) over short distances, and I can cruise comfortably at 10 mph (16 km/h) over longer distances.

- Can you guess how long I sleep every day? I sleep from as short as 10 minutes to two hours, the shortest of all mammals and I usually sleep standing up. I can also sleep laying on the ground, resting my head on my hind legs. I am more vulnerable to predators lying down.

- My heart can weigh as much as 22 pounds (10 kgs) and is approximately two feet long (61 cms.)

As a **Giraffe** my 21 inch blue tongue (53 cm) can pluck tasty morsels from high up branches.

- Did I mention I have a blue tongue or that we like to "neck"? Necking is our mating ritual when males giraffes lock necks and sometimes clash heads.

- I am very careful when I eat or drink because I must spread all four legs to reach the water or food source which sometimes makes me unstable and vulnerable to predators. I am so glad I only need to drink once every several days. Most of my water comes from the tasty plants I eat!

- I eat most of the time and, like cows, regurgitate food and chew it as cud. I eat hundreds of pounds of leaves each week and must travel miles to find enough food.

This is my smile! I am a happy **Hippopotamus** (Scientific name: *Hippopotamus amphibious*) or **hippo**, from the ancient Greek for "river horse"

- I spend most of my life in the water and mud which keeps me cool during the hottest days in **Sub-Saharan Africa.** My specific gravity allows me to sink and run along the bottom of a river or lake.

- My closest living relatives are whales and porpoises!

- My ancestors have lived on this planet about 16 million years. At night I graze on grass, and I can weigh as much as a big car (between 1 1/2 and 3 tons.)

- In spite of my short fat legs, I can outrun humans on land. I can run up to 19 miles an hour for a short distance.

- Territorial bulls preside over a stretch of river and groups of 5 to 30 females and young.

- The only animals bigger than me are the elephant, white rhino and whales.

Because of their enormous size, hippopotamuses are difficult to weigh in the wild. Most estimates of the weight come from culling operations that were carried out in the 1960s. The average weights for adult males ranged between 3,300-4,000 lbs. (1,500-1,800 kg.) Females are smaller than their male counterparts, with average weights measuring between 12,900-3,300 lbs. (300-1,500 kg.) Older males can get much larger, reaching at least 7,100 lbs. (3,200 kg) and occasionally weighing 7,900 lbs. (3,600 kg.)

I am a Red River Hog (scientific name: *Potamochoerus popcus*)

As a male Boar I have Tusks.

- As a mighty fine swine, I am strong, resourceful, and intelligent.

- I am an omnivore (an animal that eats both plants and animals.) I use my large muzzle to "root" or dig in the soil in search of food, which sometimes causes damage to the soil and brush.

- I am rarely seen away from rainforests, and generally prefer to live near rivers or swamps.

- I survive on a diet of grasses, berries, roots, insects, mollusks, small vertebrates and carrion including dead animal and plant remains. I hide in dense brush and after sunset roam with other Red River Hogs in troops searching for food.

- When I am full grown I weigh 99-250 pounds (45 to 115 kg) and stand 22 to 31 inches tall (55 to 80 cm.) From head to foot I am 39-57 inches (100 to 145 cm) and my tail is 12-18 inches long (30 to 45 cm.)

I am a Hog too! A Warthog (Scientific name: *Phacochoerus africanus*)

Don't you think I'm ugly, but cute? I am the wild side of the pig family, and live in grasslands, savannas, and woodlands in Sub-Saharan Africa (Southern Africa) along with an estimated 250,000 other Warthogs.

- My warts, although they make me look ugly, serve as protective bumps!

- I eat grasses, plants, roots, berries and other fruits, bark, fungi, insects, eggs and carrion.

- I use my tusks to dig for roots or bulbs, combat with other hogs, and in defense against predators.

- I can go without water for several months, and like my friends the rhino and hippo, I love to wallow in mud to keep cool.

- Did you know I can run at speeds of up to 30 mph (48 km/h)?

A car is named after me! I am an **Impala** (scientific name: *Aepyceros melampus*)

- I can go weeks without drinking if there is enough green fodder (food I don't have to search for, like cut plants.)

- I can jump more than 33 ft. (10 m) and 9ft.(3m) high.

- When frightened, our entire herd starts leaping about to confuse the predator.

- When escaping from predators, I release a scent from the glands on my heels, which can help us stay together as a group. This is done by performing a high kick of my hind legs.

- We are one of the most abundant antelopes in Africa, and live in single-sex herds.

I am a **Jaguar**, (scientific name: ***Panthera onca***)

A car known for its elegant styling and sporting performance was named after me.

- Although I look really cute in this photograph, I am a lean, mean, fighting machine! I can weigh up to 350 pounds (160 kg) and reach a length of over six feet.
- My exceptionally powerful bite (the strongest bite of all felids, capable of biting down with 2,000 lb. (910 kg) is twice the strength of a lion, and the second strongest of all mammals after the spotted hyena) allows me to pierce the shells of armored reptiles.
- My legs are shorter than those of a tiger or lion, but are thick and powerful. It has been reported that without help I can drag an 800 lb. (360 kg) bull 25 feet (8m) in my jaws and pulverize the heaviest bones.
- I am covered in rosettes for camouflage. The spots vary between individual jaguars: rosettes may include one or several dots, and the shapes of the dots vary. The spots on the head and neck are generally solid, as are those on the tail, where they may merge to form a band.
- I closely resemble the leopard physically although I am usually larger and of sturdier build. My behavioral and habitat characteristics are closer to those of the tiger.
- Dense rainforest is my preferred habitat, but I am frequently found in a variety of forests, swamps, and open terrains.
- I love the water and, like my relative the tiger, love to swim.
- I am largely a solitary animal, opportunistic, and stalk-and-ambush my prey. I normally avoid humans.

I am the **Koala Bear** (scientific name: *Phascolarctos cinereus*) a Marsupial (pouched animal.)

- *Phascolarctos*, is derived from Greek word *phaskolos* "pouch" and *arktos* "bear" where I get my name Koala Bear. *Cnereus*, is Latin and means "ash-colored". Look how cute and cuddly I look, like a teddy bear. **I am not a bear**, but a member of a group of pouched animals called marsupials that raise their babies in their pouch. Other Marsupials include kangaroos, wallabies, wallaroos, wombats, possums, and opossums.

- When I am born, I am only about the size of a large jelly bean and not yet fully developed. A newborn Koala is called a Joey, and can not see or hear, but can climb!

- After six months in Mom's pouch I climb out and ride on her back.

- I am a very picky eater, and my favorite food is Eucalyptus leaves. I eat 1 to 1.5 pounds of leaves (454 to 680 g) each day. Eucalyptus leaves are poisonous to most animals, but I have special bacteria in my stomach that breaks down the eucalyptus toxic oils. My special cheek teeth (four molars), grind the tough eucalyptus leaves.

- Since I don't get many calories from eating these leaves, I conserve energy by moving slowly and sleeping as much as 20 hours each day.

- I live in coastal regions of eastern and southern Australia.

I am a Ring-tailed Lemur (scientific name: *Lemur catta*). "lemur" comes from lemurs (ghosts or spirits) from Roman mythology. I was a star in Disney's movie '*Madagascar*'.

- I am a member of an order called *Prosimians*. As a mammal, *zoologist*s define me as a primate, just like my cousins the monkeys and apes.

- Lemurs evolved independently in isolation on the island Madagascar off the coast of southeastern coast of Africa.

- I mostly eat fruit, leaves, and other plant parts and am endangered.

- We talk to one another by hooting. We also send messages with scents. As a male when I want to scare away another male, I first rub my tail on the smelly glands under my arms and wave my tail in his face. This is called a **"stink fight"**.

Can you keep a secret?

I am a **Red Lechwe**
(scientific name: *Kobus leche leche*)

- I am a medium-sized antelope, closely related to the Waterbuck. As a female (bottom photo) I have no horns.

- What secret do you think I'm telling my friend in the photograph on the left?

- Our habitat is marshlands and swamps. Within this habitat, we graze on the lush green aquatic and semi-aquatic grasses.

- We love the water and skim across the wetlands and swamp with the grace of the Gazelle. We are strong swimmers and will jump into the water without hesitation if being pursued.

- We may congregate in hundreds or thousands, although most herds number about 20-30 individuals.

- Sometimes I flatten myself on the ground to avoid detection, then suddenly take off in startled leaps and bounds.

- There are three subspecies of Lechwe in southern Africa. The Red Lechwe, Kobus leche leche, and Kafue Leehwe are found only in the Okavango **swamps** in Botswana and the Linyanti swamps of the Caprivi Strip, Namibia.

I am the **Lion** (scientific name: *Panthera leo*)
"King of Breasts" because of my strength, courage

❝ I am a female White Lioness and have no mane, but I am a great hunter!

- I evolved in Africa between 1 million and 800,000 years ago. Do you remember me from the movie, *The Lion King* ?
- As an adult male I weigh as much as 500 pounds, and am one of the most impressive cats you will ever see!
- I am a nocturnal animal, sleeping during the day and active at night.

- My loud roar strikes terror in the animal kingdom, and has earned me the reputation of being among the fiercest and strongest of all the wild creatures on earth.

- As a species we live in a pack called a **pride**. Female lions, called lionesses do the majority of the hunting. Each lioness has a different job, some chase and direct prey, others ambush. Even though they do the hunting I am the first to eat because I am the leader of the pride, and it is my role to defend our territory.

- **Photo to the left - White lions.** We were extinct in the wild but only recently were reintroduced into our natural habitat. We are not albinos, but are a genetic rarity. As you can see, we are incredibly playful and affectionate.

We are **Meerkats** (scientific name: *Suricata suricatta*) members of the mongoose family.

- Meerkats are very sociable and spend much of our time basking in the sun and grooming.

- We love to eat insects and live in southern Africa.

- We work as a team to protect our families against predators.

I am a **M**onkey, a Japanese Macaque,
(scientific name: *Macaca fuscata*).
I am commonly referred to as a Snow Monkey
because I can make snowballs.

- When I search for food, I store it in my cheeks.
- My family (called a **troop**) consists of about 20-30 individuals.
- We are very sociable, groom each other, and share the job of raising our babies.

We are monkeys too, and come in all sizes and shapes!

- We live all over the world, our habitat is tropical rain forest, islands, steppes (grassland), savannas, and we even live in cities. Unlike the savanna where the temperature is hot, we survive the colder mountain weather in the winter months.
- We use our arms, legs, and some of us even use our tails to run, jump, climb, and swing though the trees.
- Our diet consists of flowers, fruits and vegetables, nuts, leaves, seeds, insects, birds' eggs, spiders, and small mammals.
- Our favorite place to live is the tropical rain forest, which is quickly disappearing as man cuts and burns the forest to make his own place to live and work.

My ancestors have lived on this planet with the first dinosaurs about 200 million years ago! Who am I?   Nile Crocodile.

I am the Nile Crocodile (scientific name: *Crocodylus niloticus*)

I am an African crocodile, one of the oldest living creatures on earth. Crocodiles appeared with the first dinosaurs about 200 million years ago, and have virtually remained unchanged.

- As a species, we live mainly in East Africa and are found in rivers, lakes, marshes, and dams, but have also adapted to life in caves. The largest and most dangerous crocodile lives in Australia and is known as "saltie". Unlike other crocodiles it lives in both saltwater and freshwater.

- I normally crawl along on my belly, but as you can see in this photograph, I can **"high walk"** with my trunk raised above the ground.

- I am capable of bursts of speeds, reaching up to 7.5 to 8.7 mph (12 to 14 km/h), but can swim about 18 to 22 mph (30 to 35 km/h.) My species moves quickly by moving our bodies and tails in a sinuous fashion (serpentine or wavy/winding motion.)

- I am able to stay underwater for up to 30 minutes and can hold my breath up to two hours while lying motionless in the water, waiting to ambush my next meal.

- When I do eat, I can eat up to half my body weight as much as 850 pounds (375 kg) at a time; **what a huge meal**! Since I move very little, a meal like this could satisfy me for several months. Because of my ectothermic metabolism (internal heat that remains practically constant), I can survive for long periods between meals. I get most of my heat from external sources such as sunlight; that's why I sunbathe.

- My only real threat is another crocodile, adult hippo, and occasionally a Siberian tiger .

- Females nest in November or December and prefer sandy shores, dry stream beds, or riverbanks. She digs a hole a few feet from the bank and up to 20 inches (500 mm) deep, and lays an average of 50 eggs. Her eggs resemble chicken eggs, but have a much thinner shell. This sounds like a lot of eggs but many of her young do not survive.

What am I? An **Okapi** (scientific name: *Okapia johnstoni*)

My home is in the blue area on the map - Congo in Central Africa.

- I am an herbivore (adapted to eat plant-based foods), and eat tree leaves, buds, grass, fruit, and fungi. Many of the plant species I eat are poisonous to humans.

- I prefer altitudes of 546 –1,093 yards (500 to 1,000 m), but sometimes venture above this altitude in the mountain and cloud forest (which gains its moisture from clouds and fog.)

- As you can see by the photo from behind, I resemble the zebra with my striped markings, but I am most closely related to the giraffe only my neck is much shorter. Like the giraffe I have a flexible blue tongue that I use to strip leaves and buds from trees.

- Because there is a considerable amount of rain in these forests, I have an oily, velvety coat of fur that repels the water and also serves as a camouflage.

- There are approximately 10,000—20,000 of us in the wild.

- Although I am not classified as endangered, I am threatened by habitat destruction and poaching.

- Carved images of me have been found in Ancient Egypt.

I am a **Scimitar Oryx** of North Africa (scientific name: *Oryx dammah*).

How do you like my magnificent horns?

- My horns can be lethal. I have been known to kill lions with my horns.

- Both males and females have permanent horns.

- All Oryx species prefer near desert conditions and can survive without water for long periods.

- Our species live in herds of up to 600 animals. Newborn calves are able to run with the herd immediately after birth.

- We feed in early morning and late afternoon, our diet mainly consists of coarse grasses and boughs from thorny shrubs. In desert areas we consume thick leaved plants, wild melons, and roots and tubers which we dig out of the ground.

- I am thought to be extinct in the Wild.

I am a **Red Panda** (scientific name: *Ailurus fulgens*) and live in the eastern Himalayas and southwestern China.

- Like my friend the Giant Panda Bear, I eat mainly bamboo, but unlike him I am an omnivore and also eat eggs, birds, insects, and small mammals.

- I am generally quiet except for some tweeting, and whistling communication sounds.

- I am much smaller than my cousin the Giant Panda and I am red, he is white and black, like him I am an excellent climber.

I am a **Giant Panda** (scientific name: *Ailuropoda melanoleuca*)

- 99% of my diet is bamboo and I eat half the day, a full 12 out of every 24 hours. I am often seen eating in this relaxed sitting posture, with my hind legs stretched out before me.

- I live only in remote, mountainous regions in China.

I am a skilled tree-climber and an efficient swimmer.

I am a **Przewalski horse** (scientific name: *Equus caballus przewalskii*)

- I am native to Mongolia. Today, I am the only true **Wild Horse**, however, the North American Mustang is free-roaming and protected under United States law.

- While I have not been domesticated, 1,500 Przewalski horses found worldwide live in captivity, with only about 250 living in the wild.

I am a **Quokka** (scientific name: *Setonix brachyurus*). I was given my peculiar name by the Aboriginal people living in Western Australia. I am related to kangaroos and wallabies and am a marsupial, raising babies in my pouch.

- Our species are herbivores, adapted to eat plant-based foods. We are mainly nocturnal, sleeping during the day and very active at night.

- At night we become very sociable and gather in large groups, up to 150 adults, at the waterholes.

- We mate from January to March, and after a brief pregnancy (around 4 weeks) a single baby (Joey) is born. The joey lives and is fed milk in mom's pouch for the first 26 to 30 weeks.

- You can find us on some smaller islands off the coast of Western Australia.

- We weigh between 5.5 to 11 lbs. (2.5 to 5 kg) and measure 16 to 35 inches (40 to 90 cm) long with a 9.8 to 12 in. tail (25 to 30 cm) which is shorter than our relatives the kangaroos and wallabies.

- As you can see we have a stocky build, rounded ears, and a short, broad head. Although looking rather like a very small, dumpy kangaroo, we don't just hop around, but can climb small trees and shrubs.

- We are cute, loveable, and not afraid of humans. Laws protect us from being handled by humans, the fine is $300 if you are caught, however, prosecution of the offense can result in a fine of up to $2000.

- Our natural predators are foxes and cats; fortunately there are none on the island!

- We also have the unusual ability to survive in an environment almost totally devoid (lacking) of freshwater due to some fascinating feeding and digestive adaptations.

I am a Black Rhinoceros
(scientific name: *Dicerose bicornis*)

I am the only Rhinoceros with **two horns**. The word Rhinoceros comes from the Greek *rhino* (nose) and *ceros* (horn.) I hold the world record weight at 10,000 lbs. (4,500 kg.)

- South Africa is home to 70 per cent of all remaining rhinos in the world.
- Like elephants, I am being poached and killed by humans for my horns, which are bought and sold on the black market for as much as $50,000 per kg, and which are used by some cultures for ornamental or medicinal purposes. This brutal and relentless poaching has escalated in South Africa to the point that my species is near extinction. To preserve our species, many of us now have our horns removed by conservationists to keep us from being poached. **We are an Endangered species!**

« I am an Indian Rhinoceros
(scientific name *Rhinoceros unicornis*)

- I am have only **one horn**.
- I am primarily found in parts of northeastern India and in protected areas in the Terai of Nepal.
- I am the fourth largest land animal.
- Today only about 3,000 of us live in the wild.

I am a Rhinoceros

- A large herbivore with an "**odd-toe ungulate**" (split toes that resemble hooves) Yes, I am related to horses and zebras. I can run on these toes up to 35MPH.

- I have lived on planet earth for 50 million years.

- My prehensile upper lip can pick a small leaf from a twig and even open gates and vehicle doors.

I am a Sumatran Rhinoceros (scientific name *Dicerorhinus sumatrensis*)

- Olympic gold medal winner, **Usain Bolt,** holds the world track record running 27 mph in the 100 meter race in 2012. In the race Man versus Breast, I can run up to 35 mph for short distances so don't get in my way!

- I love the mud, it's my sun block, keeps me cool, and keeps blood sucking insects away!

I am a Snow Leopard
(scientific name: *Panthera uncia*)

I am a moderately large cat native to the mountain ranges of Central Asia.

- I live in the alpine country between 10,900 and 22,000 feet (3,350-6,700m.)

- I have long thick fur, and my base color varies from smoky gray to yellowish tan, with whitish under-parts. I have dark gray to black open rosettes on my body with small spots of the same color on my head and larger spots on my legs and tail.

- Like most cats my eyes are pale green or gray.

- My ears are small and rounded, which help to minimize heat loss. My paws are wide and distribute my weight better for walking on snow. I also have fur on my paws to increase my grip on steep and unstable surfaces; it also helps to minimize heat loss. My long and flexible tail helps me maintain balance, which is very important in the rocky terrain I inhabit. My extra long tail is very thick and is one of the places I store fat. The rest of my thick fur acts like a blanket to protect me from the cold.

- I **cannot** roar because I have no larynx. My vocalizations include hisses, chuffing, mews, growls, and wailing.

- In summer, I usually live in the Tundra (an area above the tree line) on mountainous meadows and in rocky regions. I am most active at dawn and dusk.

- I live a solitary life within a well-defined home range.

I am a **Siberian Tiger** (scientific name: *Panthera tigris altaica*). I am the largest of the cat family, 11 feet long (3.35m) and weigh up to 670 pounds (306kg.) I look pretty enough to pet!

- Because man has taken over much my habitat and poaching I am an endangered animal. Poaching is the illegal taking or killing of wild plants or animals.

- My lifetime is short, I only live to be 20-26 years old.

- My species have dwindled to six, the Bengal, Siberian, Indochinese, South Chinese, Sumatran, and Malayan tigers.

- We are carnivores and mainly eat deer, wild pigs, water buffalo and antelope. We have been known to hunt sloth bears, dogs, leopards, crocodiles, pythons, monkeys and hares.

I am a **White Bengal Tiger**, unique and rare. (scientific name: *Panthera tigris*)

- I tend to be somewhat bigger than original tigers, both at birth and as fully grown adults. I am not an albino or subspecies of the tiger, but my fur is beautifully white colored with black stripes. I have blue eyes and a pink nose.

- I live in tropical lowland evergreen forests, monsoonal forests, dry thorn forests, scrub oak, birch woodlands, tall grasses, jungles, and mangrove swamps.

- The modern strain of snow white tigers came from the mating of Bhim and Sumita at the Cincinnati Zoo.

I am a **Thomson's Gazelle** (scientific name: *Eudorcas thomsonii*)

I am well known and named after explorer Joseph Thomson. Both males and females of my species have distinctive great long horns.

- Our numbers exceed 500,000 in Africa. We are recognized as the most common gazelle in East Africa and live in the savannas and grasslands. We live within straggling herds of thousands of animals.

- Because I can sprint up to 50 mph (80 km/h) and zigzag, I am not easy for predators to catch. I am chased by leopards, lions, and hyenas but I am faster and more agile in these races. I can run 15-20 minutes at maintained speed of 37 mph (60 km/h), however, I cannot win the race against the Cheetah.

- I have a fine sense of hearing and smell, and stomp my feet when disturbed to warn others.

I am a **Uakari**, specifically a **Bald Uakari** (scientific name: *Cacajao calvus*)

- My most striking features include a bald head and bright red face. My species has either red or white fur, and extra strong jaws for cracking nuts.

- I am unusual among New World monkeys because my short tail 6 to 7 inches (15-18 cm) is substantially less than my head and body length 16-17.7 inches (40-45 cm.)

- I live in the treetops in the Amazon tropical rainforests including Brazil, Colombia, Peru and Venezuela, and seldom come down. My preferred habitat is the permanently or seasonally flooded rain forests and locations near water sources, such as small rivers and lakes in the Amazon river basin.

- I am agile and active, and capable of leaping over 19.6 feet (6 meters.)

We are the Vicuña (scientific name: *Vicugna vicugna*)

We are the world's smallest camel, but can run fast, up to 30 mph (50 km/h.)

We were declared an endangered species in 1974 since there were only about 6,000 in the wild. Today, our population has recovered to about 350,000, and while conservation organizations have reduced its level of threat, they still call for active conservation programs to protect our population levels from poaching, habitat loss, and other threats.

We live high in the Andes Mountains on barren mountain slopes up to 16,500 ft. (5,000 m.)

- We are believed to share a wild ancestry with domesticated alpacas, which are raised for their fiber. We are rounded up by the villagers each year for the small amounts of extremely fine wool, which is very expensive because our coat can only be sheared every 3 years.

- Our fur is very soft and warm. It is understood that the **Inca people highly** valued our wool, and that it was against the law for any but royalty to wear vicuña garments.

- We are very proud to be the national animal of Peru, and our emblem is used on the Peruvian coat-of-arms. A great victory for the animal kingdom.

- We are very shy animals, and are easily startled by intruders because of our extraordinary hearing.

- Our babies begin to walk after 15 minutes of being born, and within a few hours can run as fast as Mom.

- We frequently lick calcareous stones and rocks (those rich in salt), and also drink salt water. Our diet consists mainly of low grass which grow in clumps on the ground.

I am a **Walrus** (scientific name: *Odobenus rosmarus*) which means "tooth-walking sea cow."

Watch me sing!!! I don't really sing but snort, roar. whistle, grunt, bark and rasp, and tap, tap, tap. I can easily weigh 2000-3000 pounds and grow to 12 feet in length. I am a carnivorous mammal (one that eats meat) and can live to be 40 years old in the wild.

- I make noise both above and below the water.

- My whiskers (called vibrissae) are not hair but sensitive organs that help with finding food on the ocean floor as I have very poor eyesight.

- When basking in the sun, my blood vessels dilate to keep me cool but make my skin look sunburned.

- **Physical contact with other Walruses is important to me, we CRAM the beaches by the thousands.**

- Male Walrus have long tusks that can grow to 3 feet. We use them to "haul out" which is to puncture the ice to make escape holes and breathing holes. My tusks also play an important role during mating. I chase off and sometimes use my tusks to fight off other male suitors.

I am a **Blue Wildebeest** (scientific name: *Connochaetes taurinus.*) I am called Wildebeest or "wild beast," for the menacing appearance presented by my large head, shaggy mane, pointed beard, and sharp, curved horns. In fact, the wildebeest is better described as a reliable source of food for the truly menacing predators of the African savanna, like the lion.

- I am a member of the antelope family, although my heavy build and disproportionately large forequarters make me look more bovine.

- I can reach 8 feet in length (2.4 m), stand 4.5 feet tall at the shoulders (1.4 m) and weigh up to 600 pounds (272 kg.)

- Both males and females grow horns.

- My favorite habitat is the Serengeti in Tanzania and Kenya. My species travels in large herds and are active day and night, grazing constantly.

- Sometimes we group together with our friends the Zebras, especially when there is a predator in the area.

genus is Xenopus

Red-Eyed Tree Frog

My genus is **Xenopus**, there are 20 species or frogs in our genus.

I am known as the **Red Eyed Tree Frog** (scientific name: ***Agalychnis callidryas***)

- My vivid scarlet peepers may help shock predators into at least briefly questioning me as a potential meal. When disturbed, I flash my bulging red eyes and reveal my huge, webbed orange feet and bright blue and yellow flanks. This technique is called startle coloration, a type of camouflage I rely on to protect myself.

- **In the forest I remain motionless and sleep high above the ground in trees stuck to leaf bottoms by day, with my eyes closed and body markings covered. I cover my blue sides with my back legs, tuck my bright red feet under my stomach, and shut my big red eyes.** I appear almost completely green, and am well hidden among the foliage, even this grasshopper doesn't know I'm here.

- Some species of bright colored frogs are poisonous, but **not me!** I'm just interesting to look at!

- I can be found in tropical lowlands from southern Mexico, throughout Central America, and in northern South America. As a nocturnal carnivore, I hide in the rain forest canopy and ambush crickets, flies, and moths with my long, sticky tongue.

- I have soft, fragile skin on my stomach, but the skin on my back is thicker and rougher. I have three eyelids. The sticky pads on my toes are a great help when I'm leaping.

- Like other frogs, I communicate by croaking deep sounds for warnings and high sounds for mating.

I am a **Yak** (females are *Dri's* or *Nak's.*) In the wild our scientific name is ***Bos mutus.***

- I am found throughout the **Himalayan** region of south Central Asia, primarily in northern Tibet and western Qinghai.

- In the wild we form herds of 10 to 30 animals, but herds can reach several hundred. We generally avoid humans, and may rapidly flee long distances when approached.

- I have a **double-coat** to protect me from the Himalayan cold.

- I am a heavily built animal with a bulky frame, sturdy legs, and rounded cloven hooves.

- In the wild I stand about 5.2 to 7.2 ft. tall at the shoulder (1.6 to 2.2 m) and weigh 720 to 2,200 lbs. (325 –1,000 kg.) Total head and body length is 8.2 to 11 ft. **(2.5 to 3.3 m), not counting my tail which is about 3 feet long. Nak's (females) weigh about one-third less** and are about 30% smaller than males.

We are the domesticated Yak, (scientific name: *Bos grunniens*)

- We became a domestic animal 2000 years ago.

- Over time humans have domesticated large numbers of Yaks for use as pack animals and many are ridden. As a domesticated Yak, we are much smaller and reach a maximum weight of 1,300 pounds.

- Contrary to popular belief, our manure has little to no detectable odor when maintained in pastures or paddocks with adequate access to pastures and water. Our wool is naturally odor resistant.

- Because of our large domestic population a concerted effort has been undertaken to help save the vulnerable wild Yak population.

I am a **Zebra**

(scientific name: *Equus Burchellee*)

- My most fascinating and distinguishing feature is my stripes. No two Zebras look identical, our stripes are like DNA, unique to each of us.

- My favorite places to live are savannas, treeless grasslands and open woodlands.

- Our closest relatives are horses and donkeys, but we have never been truly domesticated and remain WILD!

- We groom each other by nibbling the hair on one another's back and neck.

- Our shiny coat helps us stay cool. Scientists believe our stripes help us withstand intense solar radiation.

- Some people think we are white animals with black stripes because some of us are all white on our bellies. But our background color is actually black and the white stripes and underbelly color are additions to make us beautiful (according to Embryologist, biologist who study formation, early growth, and development of living organisms.)

- Our stripes are both vertical and horizontal. Vertical on the head, neck, forequarters, and main body, with horizontal stripes on our rear and legs.

- History suggests that we developed stripes as a defense mechanism and camouflage. Our vertical striping helps us hide in high grass which is effective against our main predator, the lion, who is color blind.

- Since we are herd animals, the stripes confuse our predators.   A herd of us standing close together can look like one big animal and make it difficult to pick out just one of us to attack.

The Food Chain

The purpose of wild animals is to reproduce for the survival of the species. In the wild there is a "food chain". It is nature's way of survival. In a general definition it is when the larger or largest animal feeds on one smaller, which in turn feeds on one still smaller, etc.

All living things depend on one other to live. The food chain demonstrates how animals eat in order for their species to survive. While being food for animals higher in the food chain, these animals eat other animals or plants to survive. The food chain is a complex balance of life for wild animals. If one animal's source of food disappears, such as from over fishing or hunting, many other animals in the food chain are impacted and may disappear.

Appendix

	Mammal	maximum recorded speed		
		(kmh)	(mph)	notes
1.	**Cheetah** - an animal built for speed. The Cheetah is indigenous to south-western Asia and Africa.	114	71	In 2009, a Cheetah from the Cincinnati Zoo set a world best time of 6.13 seconds for 100 meters.
2.	Pronghorn antelope	95	57	
3.	Blue Wildebeest (brindled gnu)	80	50	
4.	Springbok	80	50	
5.	Lion	80	50	
6.	Brown hare	77	48	
7.	Red Fox	77	48	
8.	Grant's gazelle	76	47	
9.	Thomson's gazelle	76	47	
10.	Horse	72	45	

"After a big chase, I need a nap."

White Lions

Great Websites to visit

http://animal.discovery.com/animals/wild-animal-guides.html

http://www.imax.com/borntobewild

http://environment.nationalgeographic.com/environment

http://kids.nationalgeographic.com/kids/animals/creaturefeature/

http://www.kidport.com/RefLib/Science/Animals/Animals.htm

http://www.kidport.com/RefLib/Science/FoodChain/foodChain.htm

http://www.nwf.org/Wildlife.aspx   (National Wildlife Federation)

http://www.photolib.noaa.gov

*(National Oceanic and Atmospheric Administration—**NOAA**) is a federal agency focused on the condition in the oceans and the atmosphere.*

http://www.youtube.com/watch?v=nOX_WXuq7K0

(Video of Wild Africa Trek at Disney's Animal Kingdom: An Ultimate Animal Adventure)

http://www.wildaboutphotos.smugmug.com (author's gallery)

http://www.mywildanimalfriends.com (author's website)

http://www.worldwildlife.org

Animal Glossary

Aboriginal - Is a word used to describe people who were the earliest known people on the continent of Australia.

Biologist - a scientist who studies living organisms and their relationship to their environment.

Camouflage - colors or patterns that causes an animal to resemble its environment, so that it is not noticed by potential predators, prey, or both.

Carnivorous - animals that feed on the flesh of other animals to survive.

Carotenoids - algae and crustaceans that contain pigments, this is where Flamingoes get their wonderful rosy pink color.

Carrion - refers to dead or decaying flesh of an animal or decaying plant.

Communication - the way an animal gives out information intended to influence the behavior of another animal. Communication can relate to social life, reproduction, territorial disputes, or other aspects of life.

Conflict - the act of one animal's motivation, such as attacking or being attacked, and fleeing.

Conservationist - one that practices or advocates conservation, especially natural resources.

Crustaceans - most are free living aquatic animals such as crabs, lobsters, shrimp, krill, and barnacles.

Cud - the portion of food that an animal returns from the stomach to be chewed again.

Display - a form of visual communication in which an animal uses body postures; movements, and particular patterns on its body to communicate, usually to a member of its own species.

DNA - short for deoxyribonucleic acid, a very long molecule made up of small individual units. DNA is found in the cells of all animals and spells out the genes of the animal.

Deforestation - the removal of a stand of trees where the land thereafter is converted for a non-forest use.

Dominance - within a group of animals some members have a higher status. With higher status they are given access to resources like food and mates. Status is sometimes determined by fighting or ritualized displays.

Emotion - refers to feeling of being angry, fearful, or happy for example. Some body and behavior changes are associated with these feelings.

Environmentalist - a person who advocates or works to protect the air, water, animals, plants, and other natural resources from destruction, deforestation, and pollution or its effects.

Evolution - changes in the genetic makeup between one generation of species to the next.

Felids - the biological family of the cats.

Genus - a primary category in the classification of animals

Grooming - a behavior that keeps what covers the body of an animal, such as fur or feathers, in good condition. Social animal sometimes groom each other, or even another species.

Habitat - the place, or type of place, where the animal lives naturally. Habitats include forests, grasslands, deserts, and coral reefs.

Herbivores - animals adapted to eating plants, like deer, grasshoppers, and rabbits.

Herd - a large group of animals that feed and travel together.

Hooves - the horny covering protecting the feet in certain animals, as the ox and horse.

Horn - a hard pointed growth on a mammal's head which is usually hollow.

Jackfruit - a species of tree in the mulberry family native to the South and Southeast Asia.

Indigenous - originating and living or occurring naturally in an area or environment.

Instinct - a genetically inherited ability enabling an animal to act in a particular way without having to learn it first, for example build a nest.

Insulation - something that slows down the heat or cold. Animals use fur, feathers, color of their skin, and fat as insulation to help keep them warm or cool.

Intelligence - an ability the think and solve problems in a way that involves understanding. Communication is a form of intelligence.

Animal Glossary

Invertebrates - animal species that do not develop a backbone (also called a vertebrate or spinal column.)

Keratin - a tough protein found in hair, nails, claws, hooves, and horns.

Lifecycle - stages of the life of an animal, including birth, development, reproduction and death.

Mammal - a warm-blooded animal that feeds its young milk.

Marsupial - a mammal who develops its babies in a pouch on her abdomen.

Migration - a journey that animals make to breed or find food; most by instinct, sometimes because of a change in season or climate.

Molars - teeth that animals have in the back of their jaws which are used to crush and chew food.

Metabolize - the breaking down of carbohydrates, proteins and fat into smaller units reorganizing these units as tissue building blocks or as energy sources; and eliminating waste products in the process.

Nocturnal - an animal that is active mainly at night.

Omnivore - an animal who eats both plants and animals.

Pack - certain species of animals are social, forming communities to ensure group survival and well-being. Pack hunters are animals that work together to bring in prey

Pinnipeds - refers to marine animals that have front and rear flippers.

Pollinate - to transfer the pollen from one flower to another in the reproduction of plants, thereby enabling reproduction and sexual fertilization.

Predator - animals that live by hunting, killing, and eating others.

Prey - the animal being hunted, killed, and eaten by a predator.

Pride - a group of lions.

Primate - an animal that has hands or feet that can grasp, and a relatively large brain.

Protected - an animal whose life or habitat is protected by law to save it from extinction.

Rain forest - a dense, tropical woodland area that gets very heavy rainfall.

Regurgitate - a normal process in animals to bring up food held in their mouth or throat, usually to feed their young. Honey is produced by process of regurgitation by Honey Bees.

Reproduction - the biological process by which new "offspring" individual organisms are produced from their "parents".

Reservation - an area of land that has been set aside for the protection or preservation a particular animals and/or habitat.

Rosettes - are rose-like marking in the animals fur, and skin on some animals.

Scales - hard flaps that cover an animals body and help protect it from attack, protects the animal from insects, and helps keep the body warmer or cooler.

Scavenger - an animal that feeds on the dead remains (carcasses) that have been left by predators.

Scent-marking - when an animal dispenses an odor into the environment, or sometimes onto itself or another animal to mark their territory or attract a mate. Usually chemical signal with urine.

Snout - the protruding portion of an animal's face, consisting of its nose, mouth, and jaw.

Solitary - an animal that most likely lives alone.

Species - a single type of living animal. Members of the species all breed with each other, but normally do not breed with other species.

Territory - an area of land claimed, occupied, and defended by an animal, or group of animals.

Troop - a gathering of one kind of primate, such as monkeys.

Vertebrate - any animal with a backbone.

Zoologist - life scientists who study animals, observing them in the laboratory and in their natural habitat. Historically they give each species a *scientific name*, which consists of the animal's genus and species name. Names are in Latin and credit must be given to the scientist who first recorded the animal's existence.

Sumatran Orangutan

There are many friends and family who have been instrumental in my life and helped in some way with this book I wish to thank:

Jean Abrahamson for motivating me to pursue this dream. She is the author of *Manners Are Magic "You'll Thank Me for Telling You" Lessons on Life from Ms. Manners*

Ira A. Abrahamson, M.D. long time friend, Rotarian, and promoter of my photography.

Emory E. and Eunice DeVee Meadows for choosing me to love and raise; I am proud to say I am adopted. My parents continue to provide their love and support. Now in their 90's they celebrated their 70th wedding anniversary this year.

Hux (Huxley) Miller Jr. M.D. for keeping me healthy, as well as being a Rotary Brother, fellow photographer, and supporter.

Robert Miller for his friendship and for letting me borrow his Nikon 80-400mm lens for months on end. He too is a Rotarian friend, and fellow photographer.

Charles Pierce M.D. for being a Rotary friend and fellow photographer, always offering his support and help.

Robert H. Ruchhoff my longtime friend; a writer, historian, and my first photo instructor in 1987 at the University of Cincinnati, and author of *Kentucky's Land of the Arches.* His encouragement has been ongoing for over 20 years.

Gregory Allgire Smith for his friendship and for brainstorming the title for my series of books "*My Wild Animal Friends*" (now a registered trademark of Meadows Photography.)

Last, but most certainly not least:

Joan Meadows for being my life partner. She has provided her editing expertise, love, support, guidance, and patience on shooting assignments.

Thank you,

Bruce E. Meadows

Tarsier